101 Ways to Make Your Child Feel Special

101 Ways to Make Your Child Feel Special

VICKI LANSKY

Illustrations by Kaye Pomaranc White

CONTEMPORARY BOOKS
A TRIBUNE NEW MEDIA/EDUCATION COMPANY

Library of Congress Cataloging-in-Publication Data

Lansky, Vicki.
    101 ways to make your child feel special / Vicki Lansky.
      p.   cm.
    ISBN 0-8092-3997-3
    1. Parenting—United States—Miscellanea.   2. Parent
and child—United States—Miscellanea.   3. Self-respect in
children—Miscellanea. I. Title. II. Title: One hundred
one ways to make your child feel special.   III. Title: One
hundred one ways to make your child feel special.
HQ755.8.L353   1991
649'.1—dc20   90-24577
                                           CIP

Published by Contemporary Books, Inc.
Two Prudential Plaza, Chicago, Illinois 60601-6790
Manufactured in the United States of America
International Standard Book Number: 0-8092-3997-3

Thanks to Susan Ehrhardt of Warren, New Jersey, for contributing the 36th way to make your child feel special.

Introduction

The idea that it's important for children to feel good about themselves to help them reach their potential is rather modern. You have only to go back one or two generations to hear that praising a child or encouraging pride in a child would foster conceit and lack of humility. These were *not* feelings to be encouraged by parents in past decades.

Today, fortunately, we better understand the importance of what we now call self-esteem. A healthy attitude of pride, self-respect, and just plain liking ourselves colors the way we see the world and affects our behavior.

Our own self-esteem is related to how we think others perceive us. Since we live in an uncertain world, where relationships are always changing, we are not always sure how we are perceived. When others give us positive words about ourselves, it reinforces the good feelings we have. Negative words and punishments (even if appropriate) reinforce the negative feelings and doubts we all seem to have about ourselves.

Self-esteem is not a safe-deposit box, filled at one point in our life, locked, and there forever. Rather it is like a bucket of water with a hole in it (and some of us have larger holes in our bucket than others) that must continuously be refilled to stay at a healthy level when it's been leaking for a while. Success in life's experiences lets us refill our own buckets with feelings of self-worth. But they also are refilled by the loving and caring words and actions of those around us. It's up to us as parents to help our children know they are special so that their feelings of self-worth will help give them the confidence necessary to meet the challenges that lie ahead of them.

Vicki Lansky

When you are shopping together in the grocery store, let your child "decide" which item to buy by giving him or her a choice of two items—"this one, dear, or that one?"—either of which would be acceptable to you.

1

Cast your child's hand in plaster of paris in a pie plate or pan. Don't forget to write the name and date on the back after it fully hardens. Hang or place it in a prominent spot.

Make a family tree for your child in the shape of a triangle, with her or his name or picture at the top and the parents and grandparents branching out below.

New baby coming?

Invest in a T-shirt that says,

"I'M THE BIG BROTHER" or
"I'M THE BIG SISTER."

4

Let an older child create a family
Coat of Arms

BRICKMAN

using symbols significant to your family—
musical instruments, woodworking tools,
or athletic equipment, for example.

5

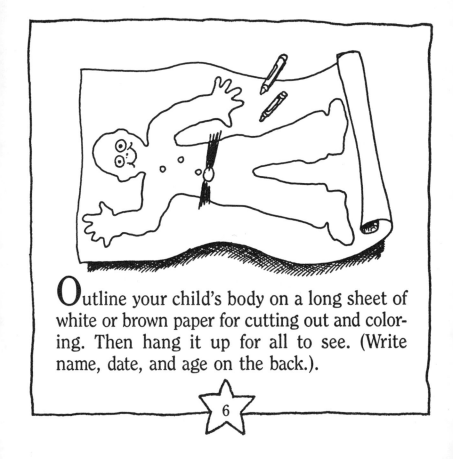

Outline your child's body on a long sheet of white or brown paper for cutting out and coloring. Then hang it up for all to see. (Write name, date, and age on the back.).

Let your child pick out a tree, bush, or perennial and help you plant it in his or her honor either annually,
perhaps on birthdays,
or for a special occasion.

7

Let the *huggie-kissy monster* (in you) attack your child from time to time.

Especially if she or he is having a bad day!

8

Remember those photo booths in airports or lobbies? Next time you pass one, invest in some
funny-face photos
of the two of you together. They will be treasured for a long time.

Fly a homemade flag, banner, or even the American flag every year on your child's birthday (or the first day of school, or the day the team wins,

or . . .)

10

List your child's special qualities on a long piece of paper and hang it—maybe even frame it—in his or her room.

Send your child off to school or day-care with the words:

It's going to be a great day!

Lie on the floor on your back, bend your knees up to your chest, and place your feet on your child's tummy. Gently lift the child, balanced on your feet, accompanied by the chant:

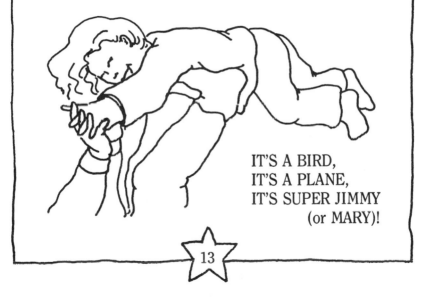

IT'S A BIRD,
IT'S A PLANE,
IT'S SUPER JIMMY
    (or MARY)!

Tell your child how nice he or she looks this morning (and every morning)—even if plaid pants are being worn with a striped shirt!

14

As soon as your child can write her or his name, make a trip to the library and register your child for a library card. Then, together, use it frequently!

Take some time when you're not in a rush (the way most of us are in the morning) to groom your child's hair. It feels wonderful to have your hair brushed or combed, even if your hair is short. It can be done at bedtime, story time, or even while watching a favorite video.

What can your child give a name to in your family? A pet, the family car, or a special tree in the yard?

MUTSY

Place an ad in the paper acknowledging your child. Many papers have special sections for this kind of love note, even if only on Valentine's Day.

18

Let your child plan an "unbirthday" party, inviting a group of friends—a silly idea that all the kids will enjoy and remember your child for.

Let your child lead a family exercise routine or a game such as:

"Simon Says"

20

Create a family newsletter from time to time (especially if a desktop publishing computer program is available to you), in which each child has her or his own column. Share copies with relatives.

21

M ake a home video or photo montage "starring" your child in daily situations—not just during special events.

Read your child's baby book with him or her and tell stories about baby and toddler days.

23

Give your child an award ("BEST DISH WASHER OF THE WEEK," for example) on occasion. Make a small ceremony out of it.

Get up extra-early one morning and take your child out to breakfast for a one-on-one encounter—"just because you want time alone" with him or her.

If your child routinely arrives home before you do, leave a WELCOME HOME note or a message to be played on a tape recorder.

26

Visit your child periodically at school or day-care at lunchtime, if possible, and share the meal.

27

TO: MY KID
259 Our Street
Favorite Town, USA
95109

I found an extra hug today and wanted to send it off your way...

Send your child
a funny greeting card by
mail. You can make it, or you
can buy one especially designed for kids.

28

Use stickers and prize ribbons in recognition of your child's help at home. Buy them at a school-supply store.

Ask your child's opinion of the solution to a problem. A child's judgment needs to be exercised, starting with simple matters such as the dinner menu.

Share time with your child
in a hammock—

now there's *nice quality time!*

31

Help your child create something unique
(a clay sculpture,
a painted rock,
a holiday ornament)
as a surprise gift for the other parent.

Order (or make) personalized bookplates for your child to put in her or his own books.

This book belongs to

Donna R.

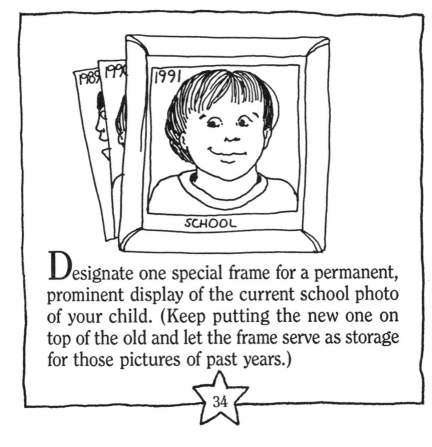

Designate one special frame for a permanent, prominent display of the current school photo of your child. (Keep putting the new one on top of the old and let the frame serve as storage for those pictures of past years.)

Help your child write and illustrate a story, fanciful or autobiographical, that you bind into a book with stiff front and back covers. (You can also check your local print shop for plastic comb bindings.)

Record your child's voice and special interests about once a year on a single tape. It's a wonderful way for your child to later hear how she or he "used to be."

Respect your child's preferences in room decorating (from picking out sheets to which posters to hang), even if you have to bite your lip to do it.

37

Dance with your child in your arms, playing your favorite music. When the child is tall enough, let him or her stand on your feet as you go through the dance motions.

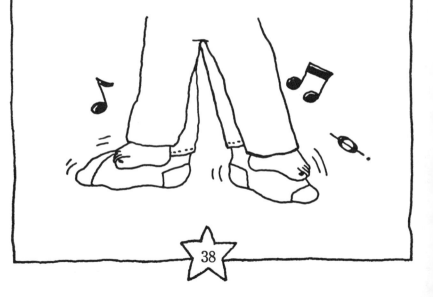

Order a copy of the newspaper that was published on your child's birth date the next time you see one advertised in a catalog or magazine, and give it as a special birthday gift.

Make handprint cookies.

Cut around your child's hand on cookie dough with a blunt knife, and after the cookies are baked let him or her decorate the "hand" with a frosting tube.

Children love to hear stories about themselves before they were born, especially how you chose their names.

Don't forget to tell them about the names you almost used and then discarded!

Let your small child give you a back massage
by walking up and down
your back,
taking small
steps (and feeling
pretty powerful
doing it).

Make your child's interest a family hobby. Following his or her lead in rock hunting, ice hockey, or coin collecting can open new interests for all while quietly emphasizing the significance of your child's ideas.

As you read a story to your child, let him or her "illustrate" it with markers on paper. When you tell a story from memory, the child will enjoy watching *you* create the illustrations.

Spend an afternoon teaching your child to whistle through her or his fingers on a piece of grass, to blow a bubble,

to play jacks,

to make a daisy chain, or to perform any of your other childhood activities.

Next time you shampoo your child's hair, use the lather to create fancy "hairdos" he or she can admire with a hand-held, unbreakable mirror. (When it's time to dry off, use a towel to create an exotic turban!)

46

Personalized name-and-address stickers or tape can be purchased or made (you can type your child's first and last names on a piece of paper, cut it out, and use transparent tape to affix

the paper to a pencil) for a child to clearly mark what is hers or his. Name-and-address stickers can also be sent to grandparents to encourage them to use when writing to their grandchildren.

Create a special bedtime ritual that you follow in addition to reading a book or sharing talk about the day. Consider a silly good-night rhyme such as:

Good night
Sleep tight
Don't let the bedbugs bite
And if they do
Grab a shoe
And hit them till they're black and blue

Do show up at your child's practices, performances, and recitals. A child *will* remember any event you *don't* attend.

Children like to hear their names often in conversation, but be careful about using a nickname unless your child really likes it. Use your child's name in other ways, too—spelled out in wooden letters on the wall of his or her room, for example, or as a nameplate on the bedroom door.

Bring a snack with you when you pick up your child from school or daycare—it's a visible sign that you were thinking of your child.

51

E very child *loves*

to have a ver-r-r-y long piggyback ride.

52

Give your child a hug every day, every time he or she returns home from school or any other activity as a family tradition.

53

Look at old
snapshots
with your child,
taking advantage
of the
opportunity
to sit close
together.

Talk about your childhood—children love to
hear about "the old days." (Encourage this
activity with extended family members such as
visiting grandparents, aunts, and uncles, too.)

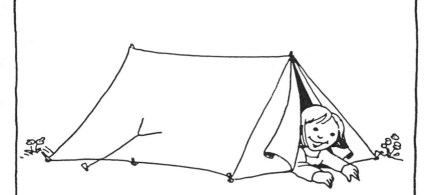

Plan a special trip together once a year. It can be any kind of outing, a meal out, a weekend camping trip, or a vacation. Let your child help pick the place and plan the activities.

55

Let your child plant her or his own garden next to yours, using either seeds or already-started plants.

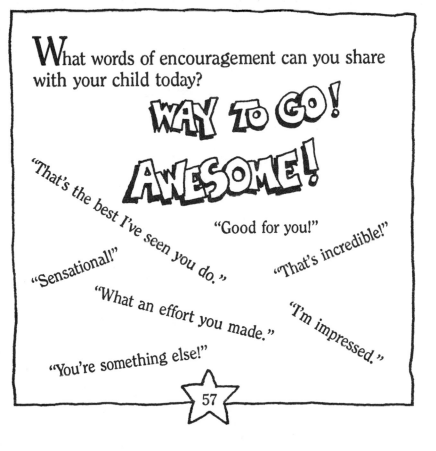

What words of encouragement can you share with your child today?

WAY TO GO!

AWESOME!

"That's the best I've seen you do."

"Good for you!"

"That's incredible!"

"Sensational!"

"What an effort you made."

"I'm impressed."

"You're something else!"

57

Teach your child a few simple riddles and jokes to tell friends so that she or he can get a good laugh. Creating a laugh gives kids a powerful and wonderful feeling.

Help your child learn to do his or her own laundry and enjoy some private time together at the same time. Kids love to run those powerful machines—just not alone.

Don't cut your child's hair yourself when he or she is old enough to request a professional cut or when the act of barbering becomes a source of family conflict.

Send an anonymous note to your child from a secret admirer.

(Don't admit to being the sender.)

When you find a comic strip or cartoon that is relevant to your child in some way, photocopy it with a cut-out picture of your child's head placed over that favorite comic character's head.

Have a poster made from a blown-up favorite photo of your child to decorate her or his room.

Your photo developer may offer the service, and it is often available through catalogs or magazine ads.

63

Clip and save articles of interest to your child (as opposed to those *you* would like him or her to read.

MONKEY HAS TWIN BABIES AT ZOO!

Set aside an evening for watching family home movies or videotapes.

Push your child on a swing for as long as he or she likes . . .

. . . or at least longer than you really feel like doing it.

66

Play one-on-one "Hide and Seek."

When found, the child must submit to a big *hug* and *kiss*.

67

Spend time in your bedroom going through your jewelry box with your child. Kids love to handle and try on jewelry and to hear the stories that come with each piece.

68

Thumb wrestle your child,
giving whatever handicap
is appropriate.

Without a shopping agenda or tight time-table, take a bus or train ride downtown with your child.

70

Make up a crossword puzzle for your child, with clues emphasizing key facts and interests in her or his life.

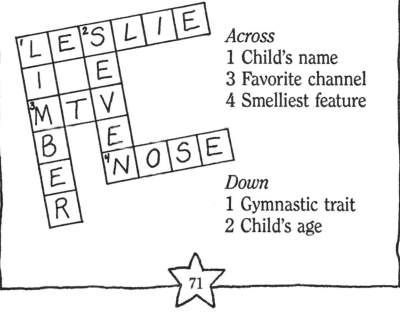

Across
1 Child's name
3 Favorite channel
4 Smelliest feature

Down
1 Gymnastic trait
2 Child's age

71

A NIGHTLY RAKE!

Five minutes of back scratching, once in bed, is always a special treat!

Spend an afternoon together rearranging and organizing your child's room according to his or her recommendations.

73

Let your child choose one special day when he or she will be King or Queen for the whole 24 hours, having the choice of TV shows, no household chores to do, the preferred seat in the car—every possible heart's desire.

Give your child a standing ovation (from family, friends, or both) at mealtime or any time it's appropriate to acknowledge a special deed.

Draw a picture or write a loving message on the napkin you put in your child's lunch box.

Purchase or make personalized stationery or notepads for your child.

Every child should have the chance to have a lemonade stand at least once. Let your child determine the type of lemonade, the kind of cups, and the number of chairs to be used. Even if the profits are low, it's a wonderful photo opportunity.

78

Ask your employer for permission to have your child visit Mom or Dad at the office. Your child will like being able to picture where you are and what you do all day.

Go shopping with your child to buy a personal diary in which she or he can record daily happenings (a good way to encourage future journal writing).

Personalize your child's favorite meal or dish with his or her name:

> a "Jenny Dog,"
> a "Johnwich,"
> or "Mikaroni" (macaroni) and cheese.

Point out to your child how he or she resembles your spouse, such as naturally curly hair, dimples, love for reading. Always use positive things (even for an ex) for your child feels "part" of that parent as well as of you.

Encourage your child to write a favorite author a fan letter, which can be addressed in care of the book's publisher.
(You may take the child's dictation.)

Authors often respond warmly to such fan mail, and your child may be the thrilled recipient of a personal response.

Performance charts show visible signs of success to the whole family. Stars or bright stickers can be used on a chart to show anything from potty-training successes to the daily act of bed making.

Put together a dress-up box with clothes you'd otherwise toss or fun items from garage sales. It's fun to dress up and act out characters or just to play at being grown-up.

Having your own wallet is a sign of growing up. At any age a child can carry one with a social security card (make one if necessary), a copy of a health insurance card, a business card, and family photos. This can be a good place to store that library card, too.

Create a surprise WANTED poster to put up in a visible place. Paste on a photo and print the following:

Don't throw out your child's "stuff" (art-work, souvenirs, party prizes, and such) unilaterally. Go through it together to see what should be tossed, and you'll find yourself spending some nice quality time with your child in the process.

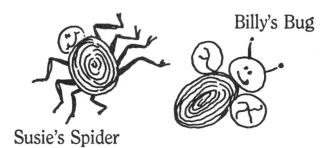

Billy's Bug

Susie's Spider

"Fingerprint" your child, using a water-based paint and paper. Then let your child draw his or her own thumbprint creatures, giving them names when appropriate. Consider framing the best ones (make sure to put the date on the back).

Take the time to play a board or card game of your child's choice. (To keep a checkers game challenging and "fair," turn the board after every third move.)

Give your child the chance to experience the feeling of self-worth that comes from helping someone else:

adopt a senior;
visit a nursing home;
donate a gift to an organization that helps less fortunate children at holiday time; join in a neighborhood spring clean-up project.

Photocopy money (in reduced size) with a cut-out photo of your child placed over the president's picture to use in games like Monopoly. You might use your different children for the different denominations.

For a child not yet reading, tape-record your reading of your child's favorite books, so that he or she can play the stories back on demand (which might be when you're not around).

AND THEY LIVED HAPPILY EVER AFTER.

93

Buy a school record book or create one by putting at least 12 stiff page dividers with pockets into a three-ring binder. Each year let your child use the appropriate page to save her or his annual school picture, to print or write her or his name to record writing progress from year to year. List items such as your child's best friends, teacher's name, and favorite activities. Use the pockets to hold report cards, awards, and the like.

Spend time cooking together.
Whether you prepare a meal
or decorate a cake,

such relaxed, shared kitchen time
is always memorable and special
for a child.

95

Use old Halloween makeup for an occasional face-painting event, just for the fun of it. Designs can be as simple as a flower on the cheek to celebrate May Day or as full-blown as a clown face.

No child is ever too old
or too big
to be hugged.

(In private, even a teen may welcome this
show of affection.)

Create a secret, special message box or book for just you and your child. It can hold records of events, questions, love messages. When your

child is old enough to write alone, you can "send" messages back and forth through the box or book.

Encourage your child's expertise in any area in which he or she shows an interest. Developing a passion—for poetry, baseball, fixing things—can bring lifelong pleasure and personal satisfaction.

Remember how great it was to get money—with no strings attached? Surprise your child at birthday time with the gift of one crisp new dollar bill for each year of her or his age.

Birthday Bucks

Listen, really listen, when your child talks to you. There is nothing more significant than being paid attention to (and, therefore, being valued) to make one feel special.

101

Use the following pages to jot down your child's accomplishments, likes and dislikes, qualities, or goals—you can refer to your notes later, at a time you want to make your child feel extra-special. Or perhaps you have ideas for new ways to enhance her or his self-esteem. (Feel free to send me your ideas—see address, page 107!)

Child's name _____

104

Child's name _____

Child's name _____

106

Do you have a favorite way you show your child he or she is special? Send any ideas you'd like to share to:
Vicki Lansky
c/o Practical Parenting™
Department SP
Deephaven, MN 55391

For a free catalog of Vicki Lansky's other books, just drop a note to the above address or call 1-800-255-3379.

If you enjoyed *101 Ways to Make Your Child Feel Special*, you'll also appreciate Vicki Lansky's other Contemporary classics, *101 Ways to Tell Your Child "I Love You," 101 Ways to Be a Special Mom*, and *101 Ways to Be a Special Dad*. They are available in your local bookstore.